ALL KINGS
DON'T LIVE
IN A CASTLE

A guide to strengthening the mind of the youth.

RAFFINEE A.J. GONZALEZ III

Penphoria

WRITING ON A CREATIVE HIGH

Published by Penphoria Publishing
Lawrenceville, Georgia
www.Penphoria.com

Printed by BookLogix (Alpharetta, GA, USA)
10987654321
First Edition July 2020

ISBN: 978-0-578-73346-3

Edited by Crystal Anderson
Layout and Formatting by Rochelle Mensidor
Illustrations by Saad Ejaz

DEDICATION

This book is dedicated to my brother, Desmond. You are loved, you are missed, and you continue to be a source of inspiration.

I also dedicate this book to my son, Lexington. Son, my hope is that by the time you are of age to comprehend the contents of this book, the world will have evolved from racism, abuse of power, bigotry ... a world that embraces unconditional love, respect, and unity. My request is that you take this knowledge and apply it intelligently, think independently, love unconditionally, speak up courageously, and negotiate for yourself confidently. Know that you are a Godly King who is blessed to make your home your castle ... Now go be great!

The text in this book is not meant to be an all-inclusive explanation of everything you should do in life because the world is ever-changing. However, we must keep in mind that the more things change, the more our guiding principles about life—respect, love, dignity, hard work, and family—stay the same.

TABLE OF
CONTENTS

Introduction 1

Know Thyself and Your Calling 5

Know Your History..8

Develop Your Personal Brand 12

Speak Up for Yourself...18

Manage Your Relationships Effectively 22

Deal with Authority Respectively 26

Learn How to Make and Manage Money...................31

Conclusion 36

PREFACE

ave you ever sat back and wondered why things happen to you? Or asked yourself questions like "How did I get here? What is my purpose on this earth? What will my future be like?" Or even, "How do I avoid falling victim to unfortunate circumstances and roadblocks?" If you've contemplated any of these questions, you might also be thinking strongly about what it will take to achieve great success and how to live a prosperous life.

In the likeness that soldiers are armed with weapons, equipment, and tools to keep them safe—when they go to war to defend their countries against their enemies—I believe that to be successful you must be armed with effective tools and resources to prepare yourself to fight against the forces of life. Remaining equipped will help you to stay the course along the journey to fulfilling your true purpose.

The importance of reading this book is crucial to helping you understand how to navigate effectively through some of life's peaks and valleys. Embracing new perspectives, challenging the status quo, and applying knowledge and wisdom intelligently will position you to live a fulfilled life.

What you will come to understand is that you must be in ownership of your life and refrain from allowing it to play out in anyone else's hands. With this in mind, wake up, stay woke, design your life just the way you want it, and grin, grit, and bear courageously and gracefully through its unpredictable nature. You don't have to be the type of king who lives in a castle, but you can live by kingly principles and experience and enjoy a life worth living.

INTRODUCTION

efore I moved to the other side of the country to live with my relatives, I met an older wise man who seemed to know a lot about life. The encounter was SUPER random, but I was fascinated because he spoke like a king, although he did not look or dress like one. The way he spoke reminded me of President Barack Obama, and the way he dressed reminded me of Michael B. Jordan. You know the Black guy who played Erik Killmonger in the Marvel movie Black Panther. He wasn't dressed like Killmonger but like Michael B. Jordan in real life. He was well dressed, well-groomed, well-spoken, and he looked wealthy. And, I noticed that he was driving a SUPER fancy car. I remembered what my parents and teachers taught me about "stranger danger" and to avoid sketchy people, but it was difficult for me to walk away because the man was knowledgeable and spoke with such authority and conviction. I stood at attention and listened intently. I thought to myself, "I want to be like him when I grow up."

Although a perfect stranger, he seemed interested in my future and talked to me about things that helped him become successful—things I hadn't particularly heard at home or school, or not in the way he framed them anyway. Actually, I couldn't help but keep count of how many kingly principles he shared with me. Yeah, he called them Kingly Principles and I learned about seven that day.

He told me that he cares deeply about young Black boys and how he wants us to be successful. He encouraged me to remember that, although I am still a child, I get to be intentional about designing and living my life like a king and that I did not need a physical crown, tunic, and robe to look like one. He said that my attitude and how I carry myself would make me feel like one. One of the things he suggested I do is to seek out older men in my community, including my father, who could give me some nuggets based on the seven kingly principles he shared with me. I said, "Yes, sir!" I thanked him, shook his hand firmly, and was excited to do exactly what he suggested.

Before going about my business, I tapped into my incredible memory and recapped the principles in my head. I said to myself, "I'm going to go on a journey every day for a week straight and ask different men in my community to give me one nugget that might help me to become successful." I want to acquire the knowledge and skills I'll need as an adult that I can start using now."

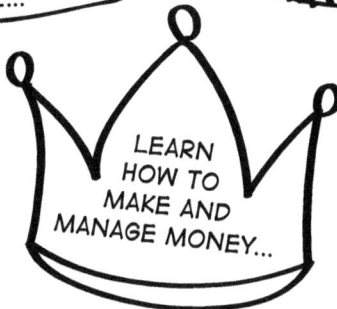

On Sunday night, while lying in my bed looking through the window and gazing at the brightest star in the sky, I couldn't help but feel tired and restless thinking about all the things that consume my day. I'm an athlete, so I get up early in the morning to condition and practice. I show up to attend early morning tutoring to receive extra support to maintain my straight-A status. I also find time to connect with my closest friends. And, I assist the school administrators and teachers with different tasks.

When I arrive home, the pressure of learning to be the man of the house, ignoring all the negativity and distractions to get my study time in, and trying to keep up with all the inconsistencies is tough. Although I am well-liked and loved by my family, friends, and teachers, I don't know if it's enough to become the man I want to be. Clearly, my plate is full. However, I realize that to achieve success the game of life will require a different type of preparation from me. "I want more out of life ... No! I need more and I deserve more."

Know Thyself and Your Calling

t's Monday morning and I am ready to tackle day one of my journey to learning more about myself and how to become an independent, successful man. As I look into the mirror while brushing my teeth, I picture myself wearing a crown and think, "What will it take for me to become the responsible king God called me to be?"

After showering, getting dressed, and cooking myself something to eat, I left the house to walk to school. I approached a middle-aged man who was watering his beautifully manicured lawn. I waived and asked him if he had a moment because I had some questions.

"Excuse me, sir!" I said "If you don't mind telling me, what do you do for a living, and are you happy?"

He shut off the water hose, turned to me—smiling from ear to ear—and asked, "What is your name young man?"

"My name is Christian, and it's very nice to meet you, sir. What is your name?" I said.

The man said, "My name is David, I'm a civil engineer, and I love what I do. I help plan, design, and oversee the construction of buildings in our city, and I make good money doing it."

I was intrigued by David's response and asked him how he knew he wanted to be an engineer. David told me he went to college and studied to learn all he could about building those big and beautiful buildings he saw around town. He went on further to explain this to me:

"Christian, as a young child and throughout your schooling, a host of people will ask you what you want to be or do when you grow up. This question is important because knowing yourself and what you are called to do is crucial to living authentically and pursuing your life with intention—based on your innate curiosity, passion, dreams, goals, and aspirations. Figure out what brings you joy and happiness and what makes you feel like you are positively contributing to the world. When you figure out what that is, you will be on your way to knowing just who you are and what your life calling is. Remember these principles and live by them daily."

Kingly Principle #1: When you look at the world and consider all its beauty, glory, and opportunity, think about what makes you come ALIVE.

Kingly Principle #2: Think about a problem in the world that makes you sad and determine if solving that problem will make you HAPPY.

Kingly Principle #3: Tap into your will, motivation, and determination to gain as much knowledge as you can to solve that problem, and allow your experiences to develop, cultivate, and ELEVATE your personal character and professional expertise.

If, doing these things brings you a sense of aliveness, happiness, and evolution, then you will most certainly come to know yourself and your calling."

I went home to reflect on David's kingly advice and pondered about those things that make me come ALIVE, the problems that I get to solve in the world that will make me HAPPY, and the knowledge and skills I will need to ELEVATE my life.

KNOW YOUR HISTORY

ay two is here already, and the alarm clock is ringing like crazy. I turned it off and thought about today's mission of learning about my history. While sitting on the edge of the bed, I realized that I don't know who I am, and I don't know anything about my parents."

I recalled a brown keepsake box I saw in the closet the other day and wondered if there was anything in it that would shed light on my family history. Learning the truth about who I am and where I come from is important to me, so I am committed to digging through that box and uncovering as many details as I can. The more I come to learn about myself—and my family's history and foundation—coupled with my undiscovered purpose, the better equipped I'll be to transform, cultivate my family's legacy, and speak proudly about it.

While completing my morning routine, I thought about moments in my life when my parents might have shared details about me as a child, themselves, and our ancestors and culture in general. I pictured them both standing over me, pointing to history books sitting on the coffee table, and instructing me to read them. I saw myself holding one of the books, but I realized that those moments never happened. I snapped out of it and accepted that it was totally up to me to learn about my true story. I plan to discover what's in that box when I arrive home from school.

I left the house, and after five minutes of walking, I saw a man sitting on a bench reading a book. I worked up the courage to sit next to him, and I struck up a conversation.

"Hello, sir!" I said.

"Hello little guy, how's it going?" he said.

"It's going okay, I guess. By the way, my name is Christian. What is your name, and what are you reading?" I said (a mouthful).

The man chuckled, closed his book, and said, "My name is Solomon, and I am reading The African Origin of Civilization written by Cheik Anta Diop." Solomon asked, "Christian, do you like to read?"

"Well, I do like to read, but I don't have very many books at home. And the kind of book you're reading, we don't learn about that stuff in school," I replied. Solomon seized the opportunity to share his wisdom with me.

"Christian, son, who you are and who you will become is largely influenced by your family history and your current social climate. Your DNA is the chemical makeup in your body; however, your life experiences, your pursuit of knowledge, and your decision making will shape who you will become. But I would reckon that before placing too great a focus on who you want to become, the importance of asking questions about things that took place during a time you can't remember, or merely things you don't know about should perhaps happen first.

The importance of evaluating your experiences (direct or indirect) and your exposure to a vast amount of information is crucial to determining how relevant and applicable all of it is to your life as you know it—and your future. Leaders from decades ago made sacrifices and created opportunities for you to enjoy the freedoms you have today. Therefore, the responsibility is yours to embark on an exploratory journey to discover and learn your history and use what knowledge and resources you have to further advance those freedoms. Son, keep these principles in mind as you set yourself on a path of growth."

Kingly Principle #1: Ask your parents, relatives, neighbors, and teachers curious questions about major and minor events that shaped the world, your country, and your community.

Kingly Principle #2: Adopt a growth mindset and expand your discovery efforts outside the walls of your home and school, and visit your local library once a week.

Kingly Principle #3: Never lean on your own understanding, and never accept only one version of history.

"Christian, if you do these things, you will accumulate a wealth of knowledge that no one can ever take from you. More than this, you will develop a sense of keenness to move about life more wisely and freely to achieve the success you desire."

As I did on Monday, I went home to reflect on what Solomon told me and made a list of questions about things I want to learn. I then asked my mother if she wouldn't mind taking me to the library every Saturday. She agreed and told me that she looked forward to the opportunity to learn with me. And about the keepsake box, instead of snooping through it without my parents' permission, I told my mom that I was curious about what was in it. She took the box from the closet, sat me down, and said, "Son, I have so much to share with you." It was as if my wish came true overnight. I was excited and eager to spend this quality time with my mother.

DEVELOP YOUR PERSONAL BRAND

I t's hump day (Wednesday), and I feel like my journey has been smooth up to now. I checked the list to see what principle was up next, and it is *Develop My Personal Brand*. I remember the first wise man telling me to focus on my personal brand and what makes me, me. What stood out to me while listening to him talk is the more I come to know myself, I must take care to develop, polish, and master my brand. Doing so will help me to discover my calling, put it to work, and cultivate my family's pedigree by doing great things in the world, making a difference, and representing my family well. And, I am ready to learn how to do just that.

Like the other days, I completed my morning routine and prepared for the day. I thought to myself, "I am not sure if getting good grades in school, being liked by my peers, and being loved by school educators is enough. I want to know if there is more I need to do to be respected and treated equally despite the color of my skin."

As I was preparing to leave the house, through the window, I noticed my grandmother walking up to the door. She was struggling to hold onto the three bags of groceries she was carrying. I ran to her aid, opened the door, and grabbed two of them from her. She couldn't refuse my help because of the impending disaster waiting to happen. My Grammy (I call her Grammy) sighed with relief and said, "Christian, thank you, grandson. You are growing into a fine, young man. You don't find many respectful and chivalrous young boys like yourself around here."

"Thank you, Grammy! Helping you is the right thing to do," I exclaimed. "But, what does it mean to be chivalrous?" I asked her.

She said, "Christian, a male figure is chivalrous when he is polite and respectful, extends courtesy, and demonstrates gentleman-like qualities toward women."

I then asked, "What other things can I do to be chivalrous?"

"Grandson, help your mother with whatever she needs, open her car door, respectfully greet your elders, and ask them if they need support with anything. Just continue to be the polite, kind, and supportive young man you already are, and it will come naturally to you," she said.

After sitting the bag of groceries down, Grammy went on to say, "Christian, who you are, how you present yourself, and how you treat people are what shapes your character and reputation—good and bad. In most cases, people will treat you the way you treat them, so be mindful of what sets you apart from everyone else." She told me to remember, "You will catch more bees with honey than you will with manure." I smirked because I knew exactly what she meant by that. I thanked my Grammy for that golden nugget.

As I proceeded on my way, my father stopped me outside our apartment and said, "Son, I saw how you helped your grandmother out. Keep up the great work! Just remember that you won't always know when other people are watching. More importantly, what you do and how you carry yourself when people aren't watching is what helps to build character and honor."

My dad and I exchanged smiles, shook hands, and he shared another principle with me before we went our separate ways. He said, "Sometimes people will never remember what you said to them, but they will remember how you made them feel. Make every interaction count and be intentional about leaving behind an inspirational and indelible legacy. By the way son, your shirt is ripped.

"Oh man, I must have ripped it while helping Grammy with the groceries. I am going to go and change real quick. Thanks, Dad! I'll see you later." I ran back into the house to change my clothes and shoes to make sure my outfit matched, and I was presentable, then went on my way.

My interactions with different people were happening rather quickly, so I just knew the next moment would be a kingly one. My dad and Grammy gave me some great advice today, so I'm excited about putting those things into practice. The day was beautiful, the air was fresh, and I felt so good on the inside. I couldn't stop smiling because I was having such a great day.

I noticed a man walking down the sidewalk who dropped his wallet. I picked it up and yelled after him, "Excuse me, sir! You dropped your wallet." I was waving my arms frantically and continued to yell at him to get his attention. If I wasn't there to see him drop it, it could have fallen into the wrong hands.

The man stopped walking, took his earbuds out, turned around and said, "Hey kid, what were you yelling back there? I couldn't hear you because I was listening to music. I saw someone in my peripheral who appeared to be waving their arms and yelling at me."

I said, "Sir, you dropped your wallet, and I wanted to make sure I gave it to you."

The man said, "Oh Lord, thank you! Oh my, what would I have done if it weren't for your kindness and honesty?! What is your name, young man?" I told him my name, and he told me his name was Paul. Paul reached into his wallet, pulled out a twenty-dollar bill, and gave it to me. He told me I deserved it and that I would grow up to be a good man of integrity. As expected, Paul did not walk away without sharing another kingly principle with me.

He said, "Christian, every day you wake up, you have to be happy with the person you see in the mirror, the decisions you make, and the behaviors you display. No matter what happens in the world, stay true to who you are and what you believe in. And remember to believe in yourself when no one else will. You are on your way to greatness, buddy!"

I was blessed to have so many wonderful interactions today, so I took a moment to reflect on what I learned and the twenty bucks I received. I didn't expect to earn money at all, but it gave me a glimpse into my future. What I realize is that I have to be intentional about putting these principles into practice to achieve the success I want, and to receive more blessings like I did today. I'm so grateful!

Kingly Principle #1 (Grammy): Be consistent and treat people the same across the board.

Kingly Principle #2 (My Dad): Be good to people and they will never forget the way you treat them and how you make them feel.

Kingly Principle #3 (Mr. Paul): Be selfless, show people they are valued, and that you don't mind taking care of their needs before your own. The more you give and take care of others, the more people will give back and take care of you.

After encountering three different people today—my dad being one of them—I learned that I'm in control of my personal brand story, the impressions I make on people, and the perceptions they will have of me. To ensure not to tarnish my brand and reputation, I must be authentic, be consistent, be good to people, and provide support to others when they need it.

Speak Up for Yourself

hursday brought on a new challenge for me. As I continue my journey on the path to shaping and molding myself into the man I desire to become, I realize that learning to respectfully speakup for myself and ask for what I want is something I'll have to master. You see, I am not the person to typically speak out and be vocal. Although many people seem to like me, I don't believe they know me, what I stand for, or what I like. I want people to truly know me, that my history is important to me, that I care about the way I present myself, and how I show up in the world. I tend not to share the same thoughts and ideas that other people have, and I don't act like my friends just to fit in. However, I want to know if being different is okay or if I should conform to the way others behave and think. My friendships are equally important to me, so I don't want to cause any problems.

After reflecting, I thought about what I could do differently before leaving the house. It came to me quickly. I wanted to change up my appearance because I planned to go out into the community to speak to different people about what they look for in a great man. I wanted to be taken seriously, so, instead of wearing my tennis shoes, I put on some black dress shoes with a black shirt and crisp jeans. After grabbing a bite to eat, I brushed my teeth, and dashed out the house.

I decided to walk in a different direction in hopes that I might meet some wise man who could answer some questions I have and teach me about how to navigate speaking up for myself. For some reason or another, this side of the neighborhood was busier and livelier; there were people everywhere. I couldn't help but notice the tall guy, who looked to be in his late twenties, speaking to everyone in front of him. He was standing on a stage-like platform, and with the microphone to his mouth, I heard him say, "My people, we've got to unite, stick together, and stand up for what is right. We are better together! We must stop the violence and stop killing our people!" I thought to myself, "WOW! This message is powerful!"

The crowd showed support by clapping and chanting in solidarity. I couldn't help but clap and chant with them. I thought he was SUPER courageous to speak up and share his message in front of all those people. I wanted to hear more, so I stuck around in hopes that I could speak to him personally. I support the man's message and agree with him—100%. When he was complete, he noticed me, jumped off the platform, and came over to introduce himself.

"Hey, little man, I'm Daniel. What's your name?" he asked.

I introduced myself and told him that I was amazed by his courage and confidence to talk to a big group of people like that and that I could never do such a thing. I know that to become a confident speaker, I must be able to speak to crowds and groups of different sizes. Daniel did not waste any time to school me.

"Christian staying quiet and not being heard is so easy. You were fearfully and wonderfully made, and God made you uniquely special to offer something different to the world. If you sit back and stay quiet, how can you present the best version of yourself—your kingship—and share your gifts with the world? Are you afraid of what people might say or think about your ideas and beliefs? Are you afraid people will think you speak and look corny? Christian, don't worry about those things and simply concentrate on being authentically you. No matter how hard someone tries they will never be 100 percent like you, and you will never be 100 percent like them. The blood that flows through your body is unique to you, and your brain and heart are made up of thoughts and feelings that are unique to you. The way you walk, talk, laugh, and play are all irreplaceable features that no one can duplicate. When deciding what is best for you, listen to that small voice inside you that urges you to say or do something. Most important, man, you have to discern when to listen to that little voice and what direction you should take. Some decisions you make in life will be tough, but if you stay true to who you are, making those choices will come a bit easier for you. In other words, to avoid being stuck in unfavorable situations or have things done to you that you don't like, think carefully about what you have to say, speak up, stand firm, and don't allow anyone to pressure you into conforming to the way they think and move."

After what seemed like forever, Daniel told me to consider if I feel strongly about what I need or want to speak up about, if I've evaluated different scenarios and still come to the same conclusion, and if I feel like I'm hurting myself by speaking up or not? As I thought about these questions, Daniel shared more kingly principles with me.

Kingly Principle #1: Failing to seize opportunities to speak up for yourself, when it matters most, can eat at you for a lifetime.

Kingly Principle #2: You will miss opportunities to effect positive change for yourself and miss out on opportunities that could help you elevate your personal and professional growth.

Kingly Principle #3: Learn to negotiate for yourself and employ effective ways to get what you want. Living a life with regrets is no fun.

MANAGE YOUR RELATIONSHIPS EFFECTIVELY

hank God it's Friday! This mission is almost over; but honestly, I am not ready for it to end. The journey of my life gets to continue because I still have a lot of growing up to do—in mind, body, and spirit, literally. I'm ready to use my voice and exercise it to manage my relationships with people in ways that serve them and me.

On my way to school, I decided that instead of looking for someone to share a positive nugget with me, I would share everything I learned so far this week with my childhood friend Joshua. I'll never forget growing up with him, how we played together at the playground often, and were teammates on the same sports teams at school. Although I consider him to be a great friend—a forever kind of a friend—I can't help but think about the times I saw him hanging out with the wrong crowd and being peer pressured into doing things that he knows are wrong.

What puzzles me is Joshua knows that I know he knows better. He also knows that I don't like it when he's hanging around the wrong crowd, so he tries not to tell me when he does. But I know him. It's tough for me because I don't want him to feel like I'm turning my back on him just because I'm on this growth path. However, I can't get caught up doing things that will cause me to lose focus, hurt me, and derail my plans to achieve the personal goals I've set for myself. He should know that I want to see him win, become successful, and live a good life.

As we walked down the street, I told Joshua about the many encounters I had with strangers this week. I wanted him to understand that knowing himself, his calling in life, and his history are all important principles to consider when trying to figure out where to start his journey of self-development.

I said to him, "Joshua, my friend, once you begin your journey, you must tap into who God created you to be and refine those attributes that will establish and cultivate your brand, or who people see and know you to be. Being aware of who you are and the brand you represent is important because people will try to view you in a different light. However, you must master and tell your own story, speak up for yourself, and let your presence be known."

We stopped at the corner of the crosswalk and waited for the traffic light to change from red to green before crossing the street. While waiting, Mr. Peter, who I always see on my way to school, called my name and power-walked toward us.

He said, "Christian, I overheard your conversation with Joshua, and I have to say I am quite impressed with the knowledge you possess. As a young man with this kind of knowledge, you will be successful when you grow up!"

I thanked Mr. Peter but told him I couldn't take all the credit and that the principles I shared with Joshua were a result of a recent conversation I had with a wise man. That initial conversation led to me having many conversations with others as I built up my courage and confidence throughout the week. What I realize was a missed opportunity is that I never asked the first wise man for his name. Perhaps, God wanted my journey to start this way.

Mr. Peter told me, "Good job, Christian! God chooses people on this earth to be messengers of wisdom, knowledge, intellect, and love. I would not be surprised if one of your callings in life is to mentor young people your age and help them to understand that they can be influenced by their environments without becoming products of their environments."

I asked, "But Mr. Peter, what exactly does that mean?"

"Christian, you can take positive and negative things around you and utilize them for good or bad purposes. The choice is yours," he explained.

Suddenly his phone rang. But before he walked away, he said, "All kings don't live in a castle."

As we walked the rest of the way to school, I began to reflect on my relationship with Joshua, Mr. Peter's last words, and three other kingly principles he shared with me.

Kingly Principle #1: Be the example you want to see when it comes to your family, friends, community, and the world.

Kingly Principle #2: Be intentional about transforming negative life events into positive life experiences that will inspire and empower those around you to do the same.

Kingly Principle #3: Achieving indelible success for your life will depend partly on your ability to connect with others, be present to their experiences, and impact their lives by way of your authenticity, credibility, example, and contribution to their well-being and personal achievements. Life isn't all about you. You were born to be blessed and to be a blessing to others.

Now, I feel like everything is starting to add up, and I am getting a clearer picture of how to apply these kingly principles.

DEAL WITH AUTHORITY RESPECTIVELY

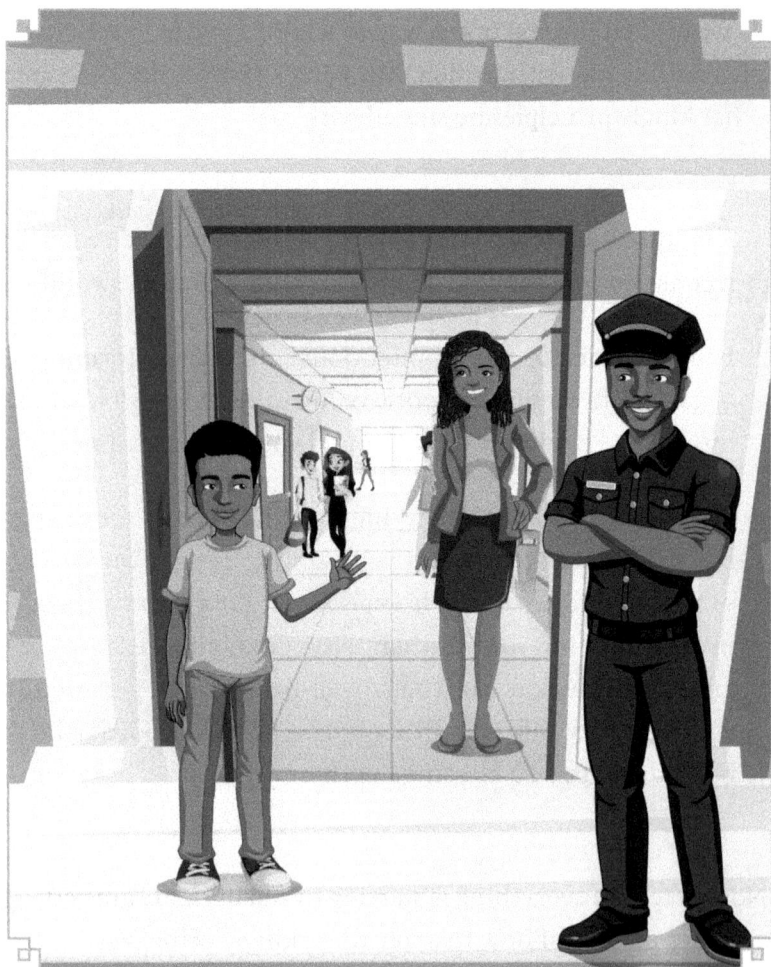

woke up excited the next day and wanted to get right to it! I realize that my week is winding down, but I have to admit that I feel a bit overwhelmed because of all that I learned so far. I'd love to give myself a break on this beautiful Saturday, to play video games, or play outside with my friends. However, I committed to this journey and want to stay the course. I want to continue gaining as much wisdom and knowledge as possible. I want to be a man of my word. Today I plan to leverage what I learned about managing relationships so that I can better understand how to deal with authority—respectfully and diplomatically.

On my way to the extra credit class I take on Saturdays, I noticed a police officer who was patrolling the area. He spotted me and expressed a look of concern, perhaps, because I was walking alone. I am not a big guy, so he probably thought, "Why is this little kid out here walking by himself with no supervision?" He parked his car, got out, and scurried towards me. At first, I felt intimidated, especially because of all the bad stuff I had been hearing about police brutality and Black men and women dying at the hands of police officers.

But, when the officer asked, "Hey buddy, are you alright?" I felt a little shy to answer but was more at ease. "Yes, sir, I am fine! I'm on my way headed to school," I said. The officer said, "Okay, be safe young man and have a good day."

As the officer turned away, I yelled out, "Wait! Can I ask you a question?"

"Sure thing!" replied the officer.

Before asking the question, I told him about my weeklong journey of self-development and the conversations I had with wise people who shared wisdom and kingly principles that will help me on my path to becoming a positive member of society. The officer was impressed and said he doesn't know many young people my age focused on self-development. I told him about the next phase of my journey and that I was looking to speak to someone about how to deal and communicate with authority. Before I could ask the question, the officer stated, "If you don't mind, I can be that person." Happily, I agreed!

"With all that is going on in our city, I realize we can solve a lot of our problems by communicating with each other," I said. In my head, I was thinking, "WOW Christian, good job! Keep using your voice to speak up. Keep up the great work." Honestly, I can't say how I became so confident in that moment, but I just blurted out what was on my mind. I just knew that I did not want to become the next Black boy who might die innocently when coming into contact with the police.

I noticed the name on his badge was Angel. I thought it to be interesting and ironic considering all the bad stuff I hear about cops. Nonetheless, I let my guard down so that he would not feel threatened in any way. Officer Angel expressed that he often sees many kids, where we live, make bad decisions and end up in unfavorable places—youth detention centers, prisons, and graveyards. He said many good people in our community and throughout the city genuinely want to help citizens, especially the youth. Sadly, he admitted that the most challenging thing about his job is contending with young people who lack self-respect and respect for authority. Young people want respect, but unfortunately, they don't earn it or know how to give it.

Officer Angel asked for my name, and I told him. He said, "Christian, at every stage in your life, there will be people responsible for you and to who you will answer. Knowing what roles you play in each other's lives will help to establish respect levels, reasonable expectations, clear boundaries, and how you should communicate with each other. Whether you're communicating with your parents, elders, teachers, or other authority figures, remember to stand up straight, make eye contact, and listen actively to what they are saying—and they should do the same. Every interaction may not be pleasant, but as long as you engage in respectful dialogue, you can gain an understanding."

I'll never forget when the officer said, "You can catch more bees with honey than you can with poop," because my Grammy said the same thing to me! There has to be some truth to this expression because I've heard it twice now in the same week. In a nutshell, to get what I want, I must embrace being kind, sweet, and pleasant. Being short, mean-spirited, and disrespectful will not produce the results I want—or none at all.

While escorting me to school, he told me not to always believe what I see on television and everything people say. He encouraged me to question everything, seek information for myself, and be open to learning from figures of authority—even if it's learning what not to do. He said that it is okay to disagree with people as long as I respectfully express my views and differences in opinion. Honestly, I learned a lot from Officer Angel, and I was happy to witness my teacher standing in the doorway to overhear the kingly principles he wanted me to know. I thought it was SUPER cool that someone who deals with bad guys daily would carve time out of his day to pour into me. I will never forget when he said that he believes in me and that he knows that I will grow up to be a great man.

Kingly Principle #1: Approach your relationship with each individual as an opportunity to gain a golden ticket that you need to advance to the next phase in your life.

Kingly Principle #2: Inevitably, the minors and majors of life will change. Be prepared to adapt to those changes and take on what life deals to you.

Kingly Principle #3: Never appear to be unteachable as there will always be information you can learn and knowledge you can acquire, even if you believe you are an expert.

Learn How to Make and Manage Money

s I approached the last day of my journey, I sat on my bed and reflected over the past week. I thought about all the lessons the many wise men poured into me. I couldn't help but feel like I needed to share this information with some of my friends who I thought could improve in many ways just like me. I also wondered if the most successful people learned these principles and in what ways they may have helped them. But one thing was missing. I needed to use all of the wisdom I received and learn how to apply it all to the talents, gifts, and abilities God blessed me with, to make money and achieve success. After a long week, I realized I was tired and dozed off.

When I woke up the next day, I got dressed and headed to the basketball court to shoot some hoops. I love to play basketball because it's a good way to exercise. Besides, I get a chance to play my favorite team sport! While shooting, I met a man named James. He seemed to be a leader and stood out among everyone at the courts. Before starting the next game, I said, "Excuse me, Mister. I'm working on a project, and I would like to know if you can answer a question for me?" He replied, "Sure thing, little man. What's up?"

"How do people become millionaires and billionaires?" I asked. He smirked and was surprised that I asked that question while playing basketball. Nevertheless, he thanked me for asking him and said that he loves to speak with young people and to give them life advice. It seems like I picked the perfect person to share some nuggets with me. He did not hesitate to say, "The first thing you have to do is work very hard."

I said, "Yeah, my dad told me the same thing but not much more than that. By the way, my name is Christian, and my project requires me to gain information that would help me develop into a knowledgeable and positive member of society. Throughout the week, I learned about six different principles, but I did not learn anything about money. Mr. James, when and how did you learn about money? Perhaps, do you have any pieces of advice you can share with me about how to make money?"

He laughed and said, "Well, kiddo, money makes the world go round, and the sooner you gain an understanding of what that means and how it can impact your life, the better off you will be. Understanding how money works is one key to building wealth. Notice that I did not say that it is the key to getting rich. Rich is a destination, and it is a status you can obtain by working hard and being disciplined. Heck, some people are just extremely lucky and get rich by chance. However, you cannot achieve wealth and adopt lazy habits. And on occasion, you have to be willing to sacrifice your free time to get ahead. Earning real money will require you to do things that others wouldn't do. And guess what, if accumulating wealth was so easy, everyone would be wealthy."

Mr. James went on to say, "Christian, becoming financially independent and acquiring wealth will require an entrepreneurial mindset, hard work, business discipline, and effective stewardship. Challenge yourself to offer a service (do something for others that makes their lives easier), provide knowledge (share information and your expertise with others), or create a solution (produce a product that solves a problem), and people will pay you accordingly.

After deciding how you want to make a living, set some goals. Better yet, your goals should be specific, measurable, attainable, realistic, and time-based (SMART). With determination and grit—in your heart, mind, body, and spirit—leverage your work ethic, build discipline, be consistent, and go hard in the paint to bring your goals to fruition. When you begin to accumulate money, I encourage you to create a budget (swear by it), plan your expenses (short- and long-term), save thirty percent of your income (make it non-negotiable) for emergencies and rainy days, and be intentional about building your credit and creditworthiness.

In simple terms, budgeting requires monitoring and tracking how you spend your money and how much you spend over time. Planning is essential for buying a house, car, and the likes, going to college or taking up a trade, investing, and securing your retirement. Saving is crucial for planning trips and vacations and weathering unexpected and difficult financial storms. And last but not least, building credit is essential for borrowing money from lenders when you don't have enough money of your own to buy what you want. By the way, if you borrow money, you must remember to pay back your loans in the shortest amount of time possible to build your creditworthiness. As long as you adopt these effective financial habits, you can live comfortably, peacefully, and prosperously."

"Christian, do you still want to play ball?" he said. I told him that I changed my mind and wanted to go home to think about the information he shared with me.

"Well, before you go, I want you to remember these three principles about making and managing money."

Kingly principle #1: Earning money comes from working. Therefore, seek age-appropriate opportunities that will allow you to work hard and earn honest money. Don't engage in shady and illegal schemes to make fast money. You will lose it just as fast as you made it, and you might find yourself in a world of trouble.

Kingly principle #2: When you start making money, master the habit of saving a portion of your earnings so that you can afford the things you want to buy as you grow older. Don't overspend just because you can.

Kingly principle #3: Understand the value of money by first budgeting for essential and critical needs, and then focus on purchasing things you want and can afford. Don't impulsively spend your hard-earned money.

Mr. James and I shook hands, and I thanked him for the wealth of knowledge he shared with me. After arriving home, I thought long and hard about what I could do to earn money. If I earn a lot of money and manage it wisely, I can buy whatever I need and some of what I want, borrow some when I am low on cash (and pay it back), help out family and friends when they need me, and give generously to good causes. I believe in myself, and I look forward to evolving into a mature, responsible, independent, and wealthy man! I'm going to be great!

CONCLUSION

hew! This week has been a whirlwind of events filled with a LOT of information! When I started this journey, I had no idea about how much I needed to know to develop and evolve into a successful young man. I am so thankful for all the nuggets and kingly principles that each wise man gave to me, mainly because I have a starting point to work on self-development. What I recognize and understand is that I must commit to doing the work, and while doing so, I can share the knowledge and wisdom I learned with others.

One recollection of my journey is listening to a wise man tell me that I get to determine my self-worth and how important my life and contribution to society will be. He stated that while moving about life with a purpose-driven attitude, I must hold my head high, carry myself with self-respect and dignity, and exude uncompromised goodness, morals, values, and pride with the utmost integrity. Beholding these wholesome qualities will help me through challenging times when my character might be tested or times when I might experience adversity and hardship. He asked me, "Christian when you look in the mirror, what or who do you see?" I told him, "I see myself." He smirked, grabbed me by my shoulders, stared me in the face, and said, "You should see a King! Son, all KINGS don't live in a castle. Now go be great!"

www.ingramcontent.com/pod-product-compliance
Lightning Source LLC
Chambersburg PA
CBHW072212090426
42740CB00012B/2493